DENALI NATIONAL PARK
AN ISLAND IN TIME

BY RICK McINTYRE

Cover, *Mt. McKinley reflected in a tundra pond.*

Inside cover, *Wonder Lake at Sunrise.*

Previous pages: *the Alaska Range; Cottongrass and a tundra pond at the foot of Mt. McKinley.*

Left, *fox kits.*

Right, *a bull caribou.*

SEQUOIA
COMMUNICATIONS

Produced by Sequoia Communications
2020 Alameda Padre Serra, Santa Barbara, CA 93103

Design by Gay Hagen / Edited by Janie Freeburg

Printed in Japan
ISBN: 0-917859-06-5
Library of Congress No. 85-063477

ACKNOWLEDGMENTS

Our appreciation for the rich lore contained in this book must first go to the rugged pioneers of Denali. Their vision created America's great wilderness park.

To Rick McIntyre and his dedication to all facets of Denali life. His unique understanding can now be shared by all who venture to the wilderness of Denali.

To the National Park Service, Superintendent Robert C. Cunningham, Chief Naturalist Doug Cuillard, plus others in the Service and ARA Outdoor World whose efforts and interest made this volume possible.

George C. Fleharty, President
ARA Outdoor World, Ltd.

PHOTO CREDITS

Jack Anderson: 70 lower. Randy Brandon/Third Eye Photography: 15; 32; 46; inside back cover top inset. Dave Buchanan: 20. Ed Cooper: front cover; inside front cover; 18; 28. Brad Ebel: 16; 64. Kim Heacox: 30 second left; 30 third left; 66 inset; 68. Johnny Johnson: 26; 30 top; 30 lower right; 36; 40; 43; 45; 50; 52; 56; 57; 61; 71; 73; 78; back flap. Julie Collins: 22. Miki Collins: 19 top. James McCann: 7; 12, 34; 74 lower; inside back cover lower inset. Rick McIntyre: front flap; 2; 4; 6; 8; 21; 42; 30 lower left; 38; 39; 44; 45 inset; 49; 54; 58; 59 inset; 62; 65; 66 top; 67; 70 top; 74 top; 75. National Park Service: 15 inset; 18 lower left; 18 lower right; 17. Photograph of the "Sourdough Party" used with permission of the Thomas Lloyd Family. William Possiel: 10; 48; 55. Roger Robinson: 76; 77. James Schultz: back cover. Kirby Shaw/Oceana Maps: 80. Jim Shives: 72. Harry Walker: inside back cover right.

CONTENTS

The Alaska Range in fall coloration.

CHAPTER ONE

DENALI: THE MOUNTAIN AND THE PARK

For untold millenia, the mountain had no name. It needed no name; it simply existed.

A time came, perhaps as recently as 12,000 years ago, when human eyes first saw the mountain. We do not know if those first nomadic, ice age people gave the peak a name. Some of their descendants eventually settled within sight of it. Athapaskan Indians of the Yukon and Tanana rivers studied the great mountain which towered above the surrounding land and thought about a name. Deciding on a word which was an unadorned description of what the mountain meant to them, they called it DENALI—translated to mean "the high one" or "the great one."

Many years later, a different group of people came to Alaska and noticed the mountain. One of them, prospector William Dickey, estimated the peak's elevation to be over 20,000 feet, making it the highest mountain on the continent. In an article for the *New York Sun* Newspaper, Dickey described his Alaskan travels and proposed that the great mountain be called Mt. McKinley. The name

Previous page, *a lush tundra landscape.*

Left, *massive Denali (Mt. McKinley).*

honored Governor William McKinley of Ohio who was running as a candidate for President of the United States. McKinley's name caught on despite the fact that the man never had any connection with the mountain.

The mountain, of course, was unaware that humans had begun to invent names for it. Names made no difference to the mountain; it simply continued to exist.

The two groups of people who had made up names for the mountain told different versions of how it came into being. Athapaskans said it was created during a great battle between two magical warriors. The raven war chief, Totson, was pursuing his enemy Yako down a mighty river. Totson threw a magic spear at his adversary but Yako turned a gigantic wave to stone and deflected the weapon. The solidified wave became the mountain called Denali.

Later people came up with a different explanation. According to their version, about 60 million years ago the collision and subsequent overlapping of two tectonic plates produced such intense heat that portions of the earth's crust began to melt. A gigantic mass of molten rock was deposited beneath the current location of the mountain. The molten material eventually solidified into granite.

Overlapping of the plates also caused the whole region to be uplifted. Granite and sedimentary rock were forced upward to form the ancestral Alaska Range. As this uplift gradually tapered off, the process of erosion slowly worked to wear down the Range. Since the core of the mountain is chiefly composed of erosion-resistant granite, it wore at a far slower rate than the surrounding sedimentary rock. A more modern period of tectonic plate collision and uplift began 2 million years ago and continues to this day. This ongoing uplift is responsible for the mountain's great height.

Which is the true story of the mountain's origin? Humans can merely speculate and wonder. Only the mountain itself knows for sure.

ESTABLISHING A NATIONAL PARK

Charles Sheldon, a noted hunter and biologist, was the first white man to extensively explore the Denali region and was also the first to suggest that it be set aside as a National Park. Sheldon made a six-week trek through the area in 1906 and returned for a much longer expedition that lasted from 1907 to 1908. During his second Denali trip, he spent the winter in a small cabin he and his guide built on the Toklat River. To Sheldon, the opportunity to see and study wildlife was the most impressive feature of the region. After leaving Denali, he used his influence as a member of the powerful Boone and Crockett Club to gather support for his proposed Denali National Park. Largely due to Sheldon's efforts, the Park became a reality in 1917. (To Sheldon's disappointment, Congress chose to call it Mt. McKinley National Park rather than Denali.)

Right, *the Toklat River area.*

Inset, *Charles Sheldon, who campaigned tirelessly for ten years to make Denali a National Park.*

THE FIRST CLIMBS

While Sheldon was campaigning for the Park, others were endeavoring to make the first ascent of Denali. In late 1909, four miners—true Alaskan "sourdoughs"— decided to climb the mountain. Quickly dubbed the Sourdough Expedition, Billy Taylor, Pete Anderson, Charley McGonagall and Tom Lloyd were not intimidated by the fact that they had never climbed a mountain before. They figured if they had survived the Alaskan winters they could do anything and left Fairbanks with complete confidence that they could conquer the mountain.

On the morning of April 6, 1910, Taylor and Anderson, the two fittest members of the party, set out for the summit from their camp at 11,000 feet. By mid-afternoon they were standing on Denali's North Peak, the peak visible from Fairbanks and their own mining claims. They had achieved their goal despite a total lack of mountaineering experience. Yet Taylor and Anderson were never credited for being first on the top of the mountain. Unfortunately for them, the North Peak is 850 feet lower than the South Peak, Denali's true summit. In fact, for several years, no one believed that these two miners had really climbed the North Peak.

Taylor and Anderson insisted their story was true, and that they had left a 14-foot spruce pole on the peak as proof. A later climber, Walter Harper, was able to validate the claim when he saw the pole, firmly placed on the North Peak. The solitary spruce pole proved that the two tough miners had done exactly what they said they had done: made the first Denali ascent.

Other parties made attempts at scaling the South Peak but none succeeded until Hudson Stuck and a party of three climbers (Harry Karstens, Robert Tatum and Walter Harper) mounted a Denali expedition in 1913. Using maps and route descriptions made by earlier groups, they ascended the Muldrow Glacier which flows down the east side of Denali. After a long and difficult climb, they reached Denali Pass, the saddle between the North and South Peaks, only 2,100 vertical feet below the summit. The high elevation, low oxygen, extreme cold and fatigue from the long expedition made that last stretch the hardest part of their climb. All four men pushed themselves to their absolute limit and succeeded in making it to the South Peak. Harper, a young Athapaskan who had worked for Stuck as a dog sled driver and interpreter, was the first to stand on the true summit of Denali.

Left, *Pioneer Ridge, last part of the Sourdough's route up Mt. McKinley.*

Below, *"The Sourdoughs" in their Sunday best. From left, McGonagall, Anderson and Taylor. Lloyd is at front.*

THE MOUNTAIN AND THE PARK

PARK RANGERS AND SLED DOGS

Harry Karstens was later appointed the first superintendent of Mt. McKinley National Park. Karstens originally came north in 1897 during the Klondike gold rush. Later he carried mail by dog sled between Fairbanks and the Kantishna gold mining district, just north of Denali. He also worked for Sheldon as a guide and packer during his two Denali trips. Few people knew Alaska or the Denali area as well as Karstens. As soon as he reported for duty, he realized he had a major problem on his hands: poaching. Poachers were killing large numbers of Dall sheep and other animals, destroying the wildlife the Park was dedicated to protect. The illegally acquired meat was sold commercially at markets in Fairbanks, to local miners and to railroad crews.

Karstens, who had many years of dog sledding experience, instituted the use of dog sled patrols to stop poaching in the vast, snow-bound Park. All of his rangers began building sleds and training dog teams. Each ranger would go out on solo winter poaching patrols for two or three months at a time, enforcing Park regulations and guarding Park boundaries. Word about the dog sledding patrols spread quickly. The poachers left the park for other parts of the Alaska territory where the laws weren't as strictly enforced.

To this day, Denali rangers still conduct regular dog sled patrols. The sled dogs have proven themselves to be a dependable means of patrolling the Park in the winter. Poaching, unfortunately, has again become a problem. In a recent winter, at least eight of the 60 to 70 wolves estimated to live on the north side of the Park were killed by aerial poachers. Rangers are also involved in a number of other responsibilities and projects. They might check on visitors skiing or dog sledding in the Park, haul out trash left in backcountry locations or conduct wildlife population studies.

Below, *an old mining camp in Kantishna.*

Right above, *dog sledding through the Denali Wilderness.*

Opposite below left, *Park Superintendent Karstens at the dog kennels he developed.*

Opposite below right, *Fanny Quigley served as nurse and cook to Kantishna miners and early Park Rangers.*

CONGRESS EXPANDS AND RENAMES THE PARK

Left, *a mountaineer on McKinley's West Buttress, a popular climbing route.*

Below, *the Muldrow Glacier, a 42-mile river of ice dangerously laced with crevasses.*

In the late 1970s, Congress considered a number of proposals to establish new National Parks in Alaska. Most of the proposals also called for an expansion of Mt. McKinley National Park to include scenic areas and critical wildlife habitats which had been left out of the original boundaries. The Alaska National Interest Lands Conservation Act was finally passed in 1980. One section of the Act partially resolved an old controversy. Recognizing the longstanding local use of

the name Denali, Congress renamed the area Denali National Park and Preserve. (Although the Park is now called Denali, the mountain is still officially Mt. McKinley. However, unofficially, most Alaskans call it Denali.) In addition to the name change, the Park was enlarged from 2 million acres (.8 million hectares) to 6 million acres (2.4 million hectares), an area slightly larger than the state of Massachusetts.

DENALI: HOME OF THE SUN

Once there were some people who thought they had discovered the secret of Denali. A small band of Athapaskan hunters were camped just to the south of Denali. At the end of one of the longest days of summer they noticed the setting sun disappear behind the western flanks of the mountain. A few hours later, the sun rose from out of Denali's eastern slopes. On returning to their village, the hunters made this report to their chief: "Surely we found the home of the sun, as we saw with our own eyes the sun go into the mountain, and saw it leave its home in the morning."

At 20,320 feet (6,194 meters), Denali (Mt. McKinley) is the highest mountain in North America. In a sense, it can also be considered the highest in the world. The lowlands on the north side of Denali are only 2,000 feet in elevation. Within just a few miles, the massive peak rises up over 18,000 feet. This colossal elevation rise surpasses all other mountains, including Mt. Everest.

Beginning at about 6,000 feet, snow and ice permanently cover the slopes of Denali. Avalanches frequently cascade down the steeper precipices such as the Wickersham Wall on the north side of the mountain. Numerous glaciers slowly but steadily slide down Denali toward the tundra. The longest one on the north side, the Muldrow, is 35 miles long and ends within a mile of the Park road.

To see Denali, you must be lucky. Clouds obscure the summit for a good portion of the summer. Visibility records kept at Eielson Visitor Center, 33 miles from the mountain, indicate that Denali is more likely to be clear during the early morning than any other time of day. The records also show that June and August are generally clearer than July.

Words and photographs cannot convey the meaning or the grandeur of Denali. There is something mystical about the mountain which sets it apart from all others. Whether you see it for only a few moments or a hundred times, its splendor will never fail to capture your sense of wonder.

Moonrise over Denali, from the North.

CHAPTER TWO

THE TUNDRA

Denali, "The Great One," is a fitting name for a mystical mountain which so dominates the surrounding land. It is also a fitting name for a National Park containing the awesome peak as well as a fascinating spectrum of tundra wildlife and plants.

From the humblest tundra flower to the mightiest grizzly bear, this land supports a vast array of life. Denali National Park was established to preserve a complete tundra ecosystem in its original pristine condition. The plants, predators and prey now interacting in the Park are the same species that lived in the area thousands of years ago. Regardless of what happens to the rest of the far North, Denali remains an island in time, the finest example of an unspoiled living tundra environment.

Denali's plants live in one of two different habitats: the taiga forest or the tundra. Taiga is a Russian word meaning "land of little sticks," descriptive of the stunted form of the forest's slow-growing trees. Taiga forest dominates the eastern end of the Park, the area around the Park Hotel and Riley Creek Campground. Dominant

Previous page, *a pair Dall rams.*

Left, *Mt. McKinley and September tundra from Wonder Lake.*

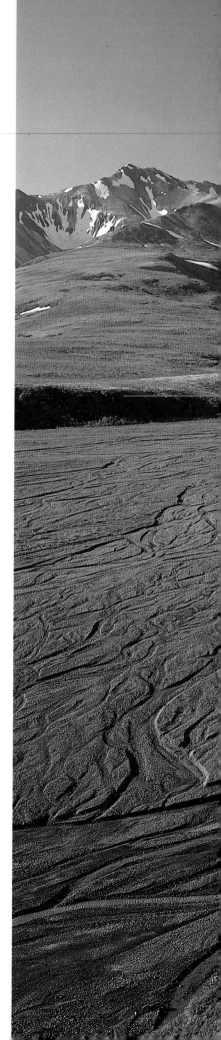

species in the taiga forest are white spruce, black spruce, aspen and balsam poplar, all growing close to the northern limits of their range.

As you travel west and gain elevation on the Park road, you will notice that the taiga forest gradually thins and then disappears. Researchers have found that trees cannot survive in areas where the average July day and night temperature is below 50 degrees F. (10°C.) The treeline in Denali is usually found at about 2700 feet (820 meters), the elevation where temperatures drop below that critical average.

Beyond the treeline lies tundra. Simply put, the word tundra describes any place where plants grow above the treeline. Tundra plants have adapted to their cold, windswept environment by becoming miniaturized. Few of them grow higher than a foot or two. Because soil absorbs and retains the warmth of the sun, the average temperature at the surface of the ground is usually warmer than the air above. Tundra plants hug the ground, the warmest and least windy zone available. The higher temperature at the surface makes all the difference to plants living at the extreme margin of their ability to survive. (You can experience this temperature difference yourself by placing your hand on the ground and then at the six-foot level. The experiment works best an hour or two after the sun has been obscured by clouds.)

Arctic poppies have developed an intriguing adaptation to the cool summer temperatures found on the tundra. With flowers shaped exactly like a radar antenna, the poppy tracks the motion of the sun across the sky. The bloom's parabolic

design reflects the sun's heat on the developing seeds within. The inner temperature of the flower may be as much as 18°F warmer than the prevailing air temperature. The increased warmth not only enables the poppy to grow and develop faster, but also attracts pollinating insects to the flower.

In addition to dealing with chilly summer conditions, tundra vegetation must also cope with a very short growing season. New growth, flowering and seed development must take place in a season only two to three months in length. The vast majority of tundra plants are perennials and many of them are evergreen. By surviving from year to year and by retaining their green leaves, they conserve what little energy they manage to manufacture each season. Some species, such as mountain avens, can actually start to photosynthesize in the spring while still covered with snow. The sunlight filtering through the snow is strong enough to activate the plants. If one growing season is colder and shorter than normal, the perennials can go into dormancy early and try to reproduce next year. Annual plants (those that start from seed each spring) find it difficult to survive such an abbreviated and unstable growing season.

One of the best places to explore, study and photograph the tundra is the area around the Eielson Visitor Center. From mid-June through late July, an explosion of white, yellow, pink, red, blue and violet flowers covers this part of the tundra. A short stroll will easily turn up scores of species and thousands of flowers—so many that it is difficult to avoid stepping on them. Many of these tundra plants are dwarfed relatives of flowers

found in the lower 48 states. Look for Alaska violet, alpine azalea, Siberian aster, wild geranium, Lapland rosebay (a rhododendron), arctic lupine, tundra rose, rock jasmine, arctic forget-me-not, dwarf fireweed and whitish gentian.

Willow is one of the most common plants of the tundra and one of the most important for both animals and people. About 22 types of willow live in Denali. Some species average only three inches in size while others may reach heights of 15 feet in favorable locations. Moose, beaver and many other plant-eating animals consume large quantities of willow. An adult moose might eat up to 60 pounds of willow leaves per day. In the winter, moose browse on willow twigs and buds. Beaver eat willow leaves and bark all summer, then collect and store vast quantities of willow branches in the fall for a winter food cache.

The native people of Alaska use willow for food as well as medicine. They eat the nutritious willow leaves raw, add them to caribou stew or store the leaves in containers filled with seal oil, preserving them for consumption the following winter. Willows are an important source of vitamin C for both humans and wildlife. One study found that a half cup of willow leaves has seven to ten times more vitamin C than an orange.

Tea made from willow bark or leaves is a respected traditional medicine of many Alaskan native tribes. Willow contains acetylsalicylic acid, the active pain-killing ingredient in aspirin. When a sick person drinks willow tea he or she is, in effect, taking aspirin and a heavy dose of vitamin C.

East Fork of the Toklat River.

THE TUNDRA

August is berry season in Denali. Blueberries, crowberries, cranberries, bearberries and soapberries by the billions are ripe and ready to be eaten. Be prepared to do a lot of bending over when you go out picking berries: like other tundra plants, they grow close to the ground. Blueberry is by far the tastiest berry for picking and eating on the spot. The others tend to be either bland or bitter but all are used by local people for making jam and jelly. The Wonder Lake area always seems to have the best-tasting berries as well as the highest density.

Grizzlies depend on the berry crop to fatten up for hibernation. The calories they get from berries enable them to gain one to two pounds daily. A bear expert once tried to estimate just how many berries a grizzly ate in a day. He spent all day watching a bear feed in a soapberry patch. By the end of the day, the bear had left behind 10 droppings in the patch. The researcher took one grizzly dropping home and started counting seeds. He

Top left, white spruce, the most common tree in taiga forest. Below, from left, arctic poppy; tundra ferns; arnica and forget-me-nots; and Denali blueberries.

[1] *Pearson, Arthur, 1975.* The Northern Interior Grizzly Bear. *Canadian Wildlife Services Report Series #34.*

estimated that 20,000 seeds were in that one scat. Since the bear had produced 10 droppings that day, it ate approximately 200,000 berries![1]

By late August and early September, the Denali tundra has entered its fall foliage season. Willows and aspens turn bright gold while dwarf birch and bearberries become a brilliant scarlet. The radiant tundra colors, contrasting with the frosty white snow on the Alaska Range, make fall Denali's most elegant season. This time of vibrant colors is over in a few short days. The tundra quickly becomes brown and drab as winter sets in. Its plants are now dormant, waiting through the long, cold and dark Denali winter for the coming of another spring and another chance at life.

On the tundra, one year is little different than the next. For Denali National Park's plants, the annual cycle of racing through the brief growing season and then suspending life for nine to ten months has continued uninterrupted since the Ice Age. Although the tundra plants expertly survive in one of Earth's most extreme climates and habitats, they are surprisingly fragile. All too often, human activity on the tundra has resulted in extensive damage to these plants.

When you visit Denali, you have the responsibility to minimize your impact on the tundra environment. Your care and concern will help insure that this great island in time will be preserved in its original condition forever.

CHAPTER THREE

DENALI'S WILDLIFE

D enali National Park is one of the greatest wildlife viewing areas in the world. Even if you are in the Park for only a single day, you are virtually guaranteed seeing grizzly bears, moose, caribou and Dall sheep. With luck, you might even spot a wolf.

But this is not a zoo. Denali's grizzlies are not zoo bears; they are not obese caricatures of what a bear should be. They will not do tricks for cookies. Their integrity and character have not been compromised by contact with humans. These bears, along with the Park's other wildlife, are freely living out their lives in their natural homes. Seeing these animals in their native land is what makes visiting Denali such a special and intense experience.

Previous page, *hiking across the open tundra.*

Left, *a caribou bull at rest.*

GRIZZLIES

There is something about a grizzly that fires our imagination. Perhaps it is because they are such large, powerful and dangerous carnivores. Perhaps it springs from the perception that when a bear stands up, it has a strangely humanlike apearance. Maybe it is because a grizzly is the ultimate symbol of pristine wilderness. Whatever the reasons, people cannot help but look upon grizzlies with a mixture of awe, fear, respect and even kinship.

There are 200 to 300 grizzlies in Denali, a population level believed stable for some time. Denali's grizzlies thrive because they have what is essential to their survival—a large tract of wild country where they are left undisturbed. Since the corridor surrounding the Park road contains extensive high-quality grizzly habitat, a number of bears are likely to be seen feeding near the road every day.

The grizzlies of Denali come in three basic colors: blond, brown and black. At the turn of the century, the blond grizzlies were thought to be a new species of bear. It is now known that blond fur is a normal color variation among the local grizzlies. Sows with black fur might have blond cubs while blond mothers might produce cubs with brown fur.

There are also black bears in Denali; since grizzlies may be black in color, it can be difficult to distinguish between the two species. Grizzlies have a prominent hump over their front shoulders and long claws. The black bear lacks that hump and has much shorter claws. Blacks are normally found in a forested environment, while grizzlies prefer the open tundra. For this reason, if you see a bear on the tundra it is almost certainly a grizzly.

As you watch Denali's grizzlies, you will probably notice that they spend most of their time feeding. A study by a University of Alaska graduate student found that one bear spent 91% of her waking time eating or looking for food.[2] This obsession for food stems from the necessity that they be sufficiently fat for their lengthy hibernation. Bears that fail to gain enough weight will not survive the winter.

Like humans, grizzlies are omnivores—they eath both plants and meat. Grizzlies prefer the more concentrated, easily digested protein in meat but find it difficult to get much meat in their diet. Under normal circumstances, they aren't quite fast enough to catch an adult caribou, aren't big enough to kill a healthy adult moose and can't climb well enough to grab a Dall sheep.

Occasionally, a bear might find an injured animal and make a kill. Recently, a wolf pack pursued and wounded a caribou bull on the Toklat River. The wolves then moved off and lay down, presumably to wait for the caribou to die. Not long after the wolves left, a grizzly sow with three cubs happened to come by. She caught the scent of blood and immediately charged the bull. He jumped up and tried to run off but his wounds prevented him from getting much more than a few hundred feet. He stopped and turned to face the grizzly. With the last of his strength, the bull tried to fend her off with his antlers. The sow reared up, grabbed him with her paws and bit into the top of his neck. She quickly pulled him down and then killed him. The grizzly family spent

Majestic grizzly.

[2]*Gebhard, James, 1982. "Annual Activities and Behavior of the Grizzly Bear Family in Northern Alaska." Masters Thesis, University of Alaska.*

the next four days feeding on the caribou.

The killing of big game is likely a rare event for most grizzlies. However, there is one animal that they can hunt with a consistently high success rate—the arctic ground squirrel. In a typical encounter, a bear will spot a squirrel on the tundra and give chase. If the squirrel manages to dive into its burrow system, the bear will skid to a halt and commence digging. The long front claws of a grizzly are the perfect tool for excavating a squirrel from its burrow. Bears have been known to spend as much as a full hour digging out one squirrel. Their persistence pays off, for over half the time they manage to catch their prey. The number of squirrels a bear eats can be amazing. A study found that one bear caught and ate close to 400 squirrels during the course of a season.

Grizzlies are always on the lookout for carcasses of animals that have died of natural causes. Bears' excellent sense of smell enables them to pick up the scent of a carcass from long distances. (Rotting meat doesn't seem to offend their taste buds; in fact, it appears that they prefer overripe meat.) Once a bear has found a carcass, it will eat its fill and then bury the remains under a mound of dirt. Covering up the meat masks its odor and makes it harder for other bears to find. To guard the carcass from scavengers, the bear will lay down and sleep nearby or it might stretch out and sleep directly on top of the remains.

Plant material makes up the vast majority, over 90%, of a Denali grizzly's diet. In the early spring, before plants have greened up, the bears concentrate on the roots of peavine. As soon as fresh vegetation becomes available, they switch

to grasses, sedges, horsetail, coltsfoot and other species. By early August, they have moved on to berries. Grizzlies are not very efficient at digesting most of these foods. A close look at a bear dropping will reveal that a good portion of the vegetation passes their system intact. Their feeding strategy is based more on quantity than quality. They eat and process huge amounts of vegetation, obtaining relatively small amounts of nutrition from each stomach load. Only by constantly eating and processing new batches can they reach the break-even point. Without huge numbers of high-calorie berries, protein-rich ground squirrels and

In the midst of a snowstorm, a grizzly digs for a groundsquirrel meal.

*The leaves and stems of the
bearflower are a grizzly delicacy.*

an occasional carcass, most grizzlies would be hard-pressed to gain enough weight to survive winter.

If all goes well, by late October or early November the grizzlies will have enough fat reserves to begin hibernation. Their dens are usually located on a north-facing hillside. A tunnel is dug straight into the hill, perhaps 10 to 12 feet long, and an enlarged sleeping chamber is constructed at the far end. The floor of the den is lined with insulating vegetation. When the time is right, the grizzly crawls inside, rolls up in a ball and falls asleep.

Some say that grizzlies are not true hibernators. Their body temperature, heart beat and respiration do not drop as low as other hibernating animals such as marmots and ground squirrels. For example, their temperature hovers in the low 90-degree range. If you define hibernation as a state where an animal's temperature stays near freezing, then grizzlies are not true hibernators. However, if hibernation is understood as a state where an animal sleeps through the entire winter, then grizzlies hibernate.

As the bears sleep, they live off their accumulated fat reserves. One pound of bear fat provides about 3,500 calories.

One of the most astonishing aspects of hibernation is that bears do not produce any waste products during their six-to-seven-month sleep. They have developed a sophisticated recycling system which reprocesses their urine and other wastes. Researchers are studying bear hibernation in hopes of understanding how this efficient recycling works and then applying the knowledge to humans with kidney problems.

Hibernation ends in April and soon after comes the time for romance. As most sows mate only every third year, there is intense competition among the male bears for the females during the breeding season. Since all mature males try to breed, it is normally only the biggest and most dominant ones who can successfully compete for a female. There has been at least one witnessed case in Denali where a large male grizzly killed a rival in a fight over a mate.

Once a female is pregnant, she puts a hold on the development of the fertilized eggs in a process known as delayed implantation. It is not until she enters her

den the following fall that the real gestation period begins. The cubs are born in the den, sometime in January. They usually number from one to three and weigh about a pound. The cubs nurse and snuggle up to their mother for warmth as she sleeps through the remainder of the winter. By April, when the family emerges from the den, the cubs may have gained from five to ten pounds from their mother's milk. It is incredible to think that a grizzly sow not only supports herself all winter off her fat deposits but also sustains up to three cubs with her milk. She does all this without ever leaving the den to eat or drink.

In Denali, grizzly families normally stay together for two and a half years. The sow then drives off her offspring, mates again and has a new set of cubs the following winter. During their first summer, the young are called spring cubs. In their second summer, they are known as yearlings. By this point, they often appear to be about half the size of their mother. When they are two and a half, they are so large that it may be hard to tell who is the mother and who are the cubs.

Whenever you are in grizzly country, such as Denali, there is a possibility that you may have a close encounter with a bear. Without a doubt, the grizzly is the most dangerous animal in North America. They *will* attack people under certain circumstances. Attacks are usually caused by what the bear perceives as a threat to itself, its cubs or its food supply. Your responsibility is to do everything you can to avoid provoking a bear.

While hiking, carefully scan the terrain for bears. If there is a bear ahead of you, wait until it leaves or take a different route. When hiking through brushy country where visibility is poor, make a lot of loud human-type sounds to alert any bears that you are coming. Singing, yelling, or loud talking all work well. Most of Denali's grizzlies seem to prefer to avoid people if given a chance. If a bear hears you coming, it will probably move out of the way without your even knowing it was there.

Be extremely careful with food while camping, both in Denali's campgrounds and in the backcountry. In campgrounds, keep your food in a hard-sided vehicle or in one of the metal lockers provided by the Park Service. On backcountry trips, borrow one of the bear-resistant food containers which the Park Service loans for free. The containers are made of a heavy plastic which is almost impossible for a bear to break. Keeping bears from your food is critical because they easily become addicted to human food. After only one or two tastes of highly salted or sugared foods, most bears will come back for more. It is your duty to make sure that you do not inadvertently cause a grizzly to develop that addiction.

Denali has a fairly good record on grizzly safety. No one has ever been killed by a bear in the Park. There have been a few people injured by grizzlies but virtually all of the incidents could be classified as provoked attacks—situations where a person deliberately or accidently got too close to a bear. If you are willing to watch for grizzlies, do what you can to avoid them and keep a clean camp there is little chance that you will have a problem with one. Check with the Park Rangers for more detailed information on dealing with bears.

Left above, *a grizzly sow with spring cubs.*

Below, *grizzly cubs are often black their first year; by their second year fur can change to brown or blond.*

DENALI'S WILDLIFE

DALL SHEEP

When Charles Sheldon first came to the Denali area in 1906, he was lured by the presence of Dall sheep. Sheldon was fascinated with these far northern relatives of bighorn sheep and wanted to study their habits. The sheep and other animals so impressed him that he resolved to turn the area into a National Park. In Sheldon's mind, giving protection to the Dall sheep was a major justification for the Park.

Dall sheep are related to bighorn but differ from them in two important physical characteristics. The fur of the bighorns ranges from a light tan to a dark brown color, while Dall sheep fur is white. In the summer, this coloration makes them stand out against dark rocks or green tundra, but during the long winter the white fur is perfect camouflage. The design of the horns also differs between the two species. The Dall rams have horns which are much narrower in diameter than a bighorn. For this reason, Dall sheep are sometimes called thinhorn sheep.

Look for Dall sheep on the high ridges on both sides of the Park road. Normally, they never stray far from the security of steep cliffs. Like all wild sheep, they are expert rock climbers. No other animal can match their climbing ability. If a predator approaches them, they quickly bound up the nearest rock face and wait for the danger to pass. Wolves and grizzlies have learned from experience that it is hopeless trying to pursue the sheep up the cliffs.

In spring and again in late summer, you might see a band of migrating sheep nervously cross the wide valleys between the higher ridges. Some of the local bands summer in the Alaska Range but almost all of them winter in the less-severe Outer Range north of the Park road which, receives up to three times less snow. Winter range snow depth is the most important limiting factor for sheep, as they must dig through the snow to forage. The energy saved by pawing through one or two feet of snow compared with three or six feet can make the difference between survival and death for many sheep.

For Dall rams, life's most important issue is dominance. They work out a dominance hierarchy or pecking order based on horn size and fighting ability. Massive horns are considered the ultimate status symbol in a band of rams. Rams with big horns do not often have to fight to prove themselves; they simply show off the size of their horns to potential rivals. Rams who realize they are smaller will defer to the larger one without a challenge. Full-fledged head butting contests usually involve animals who are equal in size: the only way they can prove who is dominant is to butt heads.

In a typical fight, the two rams will back off, turn to face each other, rear up on their hind legs and then charge at full speed. The head-on collision takes place at a combined speed of 60 mph or more! The fight is basically a pushing contest. The bigger and stronger ram proves his superiority by pushing his opponent back with the force of his blow. Since rams only fight when they are roughly even in size, it would be unusual for a fight to end at the first blow. Normally, they have to bash each other over and over again before one finally gives up. A pair of rams in Canada were seen to battle for a full 25 hours before one quit.

A Dall ewe and her lamb caught in an intimate moment.

Denali's sheep rutting season takes place in November and December, when rams seek out the ewes on their winter range. Those rams who have established themselves as dominant will usually do most of the breeding, although intense head butting contests will be necessary to settle some rivalries.

Dall lambs are born in late May, after a six-month gestation. The pregnant ewes leave their band and find secluded spots on a high cliff to give birth. Ewes have just one lamb per year—twins are very unusual. A newborn lamb will weigh about five to seven pounds and should be able to stand within the first hour. In a few days, it can match the ewe's climbing ability. Later, the mother will lead her lamb back to her band.

Lambs love to play, spending hours chasing each other, butting heads and playing tag. Games of king-of-the-mountain are held on snowbanks or ridgetops. They seem to delight in running up and down the steepest cliffs. These games are a perfect way for them to develop their agility, coordination and strength, skills which they will need to escape predators.

While the lambs are young, they often are dropped off in a "day care center." A group of several lambs will be left with an older ewe, often one who does not have any lamb of her own. The mothers then go off to feed and relax while their young are watched over by the "babysitter." After an hour or two, the lambs get hungry, call out and their mothers come back to nurse them.

Dall ewe bands are small matriarchal societies. The oldest and most experienced ewe, probably a great-grandmother, is the leader of the band. She leads not by force, but by example. Young females tend to remain in the same band as their mother for their whole lives, but young rams normally leave by their third year. They wander off and seek out a group of bachelor rams. When they first join the older rams, the three-year-olds will be at the bottom of the pecking order due to their small horn size. As they grow and mature, their ranking will gradually climb. With luck, by their seventh to tenth year they will become dominant over the others.

Both rams and ewes have horns. Unlike antlers, horns remain on the animal for its whole life and are never shed. Horns are made of keratin, the same material as human hair and fingernails. As a ram ages, he adds an annual growth ring to the outside of his horns. If you count those darkened rings you can get a fairly accurate estimate of the ram's age. Ewes also have the rings, but since their horns rarely grow longer than 12 inches it is difficult to differentiate each individual ring.

Above, *Dall sheep know where to paw through winter snow for tundra plants.*

Opposite, *naturalist Rick McIntyre observes Dall rams in their habitat.*

Inset, *Dall rams are known for their gracefully curved horns.*

MOOSE

At first glance, moose appear to be awkward, ungainly and ugly animals. They seem to be put together all wrong, like some fugitive from Alice's Wonderland. Yet, the more you see moose in their natural habitat, the more normal and logical they look. Eventually, you may come to think of them as stately, majestic and even charismatic.

The moose is Denali National Park's largest resident. Adult bulls can weigh up to 1500 pounds; cows as much as 1200 pounds. Expect to find moose in the transition areas where willow bushes intermingle with spruce. They like to feed in open brushy areas but prefer to bed down in the cover of the spruce forest. The area between the Park entrance and the Savage River contains some of the best moose habitat in Denali.

Moose calves are born in late May. Twins are common and on occasion, sets of triplets are seen. At birth, a calf might weigh about 28 pounds. During its first month, it will gain one to two pounds a day. By the second month, the calf will be adding three to five pounds daily. These growth rates make the moose the fastest growing animal in North America.

Moose feed on the nutritious mineral-rich vegetation lining Denali's ponds.

[3]*Gassaway, W.C. and J.W. Coady, 1974. "Review of Energy Requirements and Rumen Fermentations on Moose and other Ruminants." Naturaliste Canadien 101: 227-262.*

The calf stays with its mother for one full year. At that point, just before she gives birth to her next calf, the cow suddenly turns on her young, now called a yearling, and violently drives it off. The yearlings must be confused by the unexpected change in their mother's attitude toward them. For their whole lives they have been fed and protected by her, but now she aggressively chases and kicks them until they leave.

In the summer, adult moose eat 50 to 60 pounds of vegetation every day—an amount which can produce roughly twice the number of calories needed for survival.[3] As with a human, if a moose takes in more food than it needs, it will become fat. This is exactly what a moose wants to become. The bigger and fatter the better. When winter arrives, the meager willow buds and twigs available to moose cannot supply enough calories for basic body metabolism. If a moose entered the winter with no fat reserves, it would eventually die of malnutrition even if it ate full time. To survive the winter, a moose must build up thick fat layers from its summer diet.

The most exciting part of the year for moose is fall—the time of their rut. In early September, the cows tend to come together in bands, groups that may number over 20 animals. The first bull that discovers such a group will join them and try to keep the harem in his possession until the cows are ready to breed. The cows may not come into heat until early October, so the bull will have to wait for several weeks.

Almost certainly, other bulls will come by and spot the cows. The first bull, the harem master, will then try to defend what he feels is his. His first move will be to approach his rival in a slow swaggering walk. As he nears the other bull, he will stop, find a bush or small tree and demolish it with his antlers. The swagger and the destruction of the bush are meant to intimidate his opponent. Often, the other bull will run off without a fight. If he doesn't, the main event begins.

A fight between two huge bull moose is an awesome event to witness. They approach each other slowly, engage their antlers and then go to it. Every ounce of energy and power they possess is used to drive back and dominate their enemy.

Basic strength is usually the deciding factor in the fights, but two other important elements come into play. As with human boxers and wrestlers, fighting maneuvers and tricks might enable a smaller bull to win out against a larger partner. For example, if a bull can get his rival off balance for a moment, he might be able to step back, charge forward and gore him in the side. Bulls can kill each other with the sharp point of their antlers.

Aggression, perhaps what might even be called bravery or courage, is also critical, just as in human athletic contests. In order to win a fight, a bull must tolerate a certain amount of pain and injury. If he doesn't like to get hurt, he will likely give up and run off. Over the years, research-

As summer comes to a close, bull moose begin to rub off their antler velvet, becoming more interested in female companionship.

A moose-calf may seem un-chaperoned, but be assured mother is nearby.

ers in Denali have kept track of the careers of various bull moose and have found that some always seem to give up quickly while others are willing to fight to the death before yielding.

Fights between the bulls reach a peak of intensity in early October. Whoever controls the harem when the cows come into heat wins the privilege of breeding them. A large, aggressive, dominant bull may breed several dozen cows while other smaller or less aggressive bulls may completely strike out. Those bulls who do most of the breeding have proven themselves to be the strongest, fittest and healthiest males available. If they are the ones who pass their genes on to the next generation of calves, the calves will in turn be stronger and healthier.

The dominant bulls may later pay a heavy price for their breeding success. The chasing, fighting and injuries which occur during the rut, combined with the fact that they stop eating for nearly a month, causes the big bulls to deteriorate in condition by the end of the run. They enter the winter season—the most difficult time of the year—exhausted and with little fat. For this reason, the breeding bulls have a much shorter life expectancy than cows of their same age. In effect, the dominant bulls end up dying young to gain the privilege of doing a lot of breeding. You might say their philosophy of life is 'Live fast, die young and leave a good looking body.'

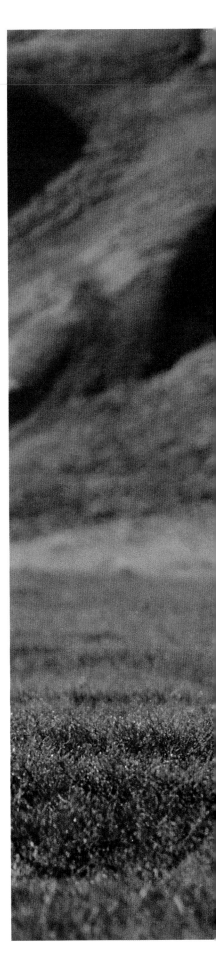

CARIBOU

Caribou are always on the move. They migrate back and forth across the Denali tundra in endless loops, stopping only for a brief rest or a quick nibble of grass. Their style of light grazing is perfectly suited to the type of slow-growing plants living on the tundra, species that cannot easily replace leaves which have been eaten. By staying on the move, the caribou prevent their forage from being overgrazed.

There was a time when Denali's caribou herds were much larger than today. In the 1930s, the Park's caribou population was estimated to be 30,000. By the mid-1970s, it had dropped to approximately 1,200. During the same period, caribou herds in other parts of Alaska were also in decline. Reasons for this population crash are not fully known. Researchers feel that a number of factors, some natural, some human-caused, combined to trigger the decline. When Congress expanded the size of Denali in 1980, it was largely to give better protection to the caribou. The northern expansion of the boundaries added critical wintering grounds to the Park. In the first five years after this expansion, the Denali caribou population doubled in size.

Like all male members of the deer family, caribou bulls grow and shed antlers every year. Caribou cows, however, are the only type of female deer with antlers. The antlers on a cow rarely exceed 18 inches in length, while caribou bulls might have racks over 4 feet high. In proportion to their body size, caribou bulls have the largest antlers in the deer family.

The antlers begin growth in March and are fully developed by late August. As with moose, the velvet covering on the caribou's antlers then needs to be shed. They accomplish this by thrashing against a bush or a tree until the velvet is completely ripped off. Blood vessels in the velvet burst in this rubbing-off process and stain the antlers a bright red color. After a few days the crimson coating fades and the antlers gradually become a tan shade. The antlers drop off after the fall rut, usually in December. The weight of the massive antlers would be a major hindrance during the winter, so they are shed and regrown the next spring. The Park Service requests that if you find any moose or caribou antlers, leave them where they are. Small animals gnaw on the antlers and recycle the calcium and other minerals back into the ecosystem.

For native people in the northern parts of Alaska, the caribou were essential to life. They provided the Inuit (Eskimo people) and Athapaskans with meat, fat, fur and tools made of bone and antlers. For many native villagers, correctly predicting the migration route of a caribou herd was a life and death matter. If the hunters managed to intercept a herd, they could kill enough animals for their people to survive the coming year. If they missed the herd, the whole village might starve.

Previous page, *caribou are almost constantly on the move to avoid over-browsing their food sources.*

Right, *a caribou family. Cows and calves as well as bulls have antlers.*

ARCTIC GROUND SQUIRRELS

The smaller animals of Denali are often overlooked in favor of the bigger species. If, however, you take the time to watch and observe the behavior of such creatures as arctic ground squirrels, hoary marmots, beaver and pikas you may find that they are just as interesting as their larger neighbors.

By far the most commonly seen animal in Denali National Park is the arctic ground squirrel. Their consistently high population offers a dependable source of food to the Park's predators. The squirrels make up about 90% of the golden eagles' diet and 50% of red foxes'.[4] Grizzlies, wolves, lynx, wolverines and Denali's other carnivores also eat large numbers of squirrels.

To provide some security from its enemies, each squirrel digs out an extensive burrow system under the tundra. Each system has numerous entrances— one old burrow was found to have 56 ways of getting in and out! A large number of entrances give the squirrel more escape options when predators appear. Also, if a bear or wolf tries to dig out one opening, the occupant may be able to sneak out a back door undetected.

Arctic ground squirrels have developed a sophisticated system of alarm calls to warn each other of approaching enemies. With some practice, you can learn to interpret the meaning of the calls. If a squirrel sees an aerial predator, such as an eagle, a single whistle note will be sounded. A ground predator causes a squirrel to give a chatter type call. This call has three notes if the enemy is approaching but switches to five notes when it comes closer. The warning calls seem to be based on where the enemy is

coming from rather than identifying the specific species of predator. On one occasion, a colony of squirrels were heard giving the aerial predator call as a hawk flew overhead. The hawk later landed near the colony and the alarm calls immediately switched to the one warning of a ground predator.

It is mainly the female squirrels who give the alarm calls. It has been found that most of the females in any colony are related to each other. The primary function of the alarm call is to warn relatives of danger. Although she may attract a predator's attention to herself by giving the call, an alarm may save the lives of a squirrel's offspring, mother, sister, or aunt. As long as the alarm warns her kin, she is willing to endanger herself. Male squirrels, on the other hand, usually disperse from their home colony at the end of their first summer, settling into a

This squirrel is warning its kin of a predator's approach.

---

[4]*Murie, Adolph, 1944*. The Wolves of Mt. McKinley. *US Government Printing Office.*

Most of the arctic ground squirrel's diet consists of vegetation and seeds.

new area where they are unrelated to their neighbors. Since a male seldom has any kin living near him, he does not give an alarm when an enemy approaches. It is not worth endangering himself just to warn his competitors.

Arctic ground squirrels prepare for hibernation by digging out a small nest at the end of a dead-end tunnel in their burrow system. The chamber is lined with dry grass for insulation. Depending on its age and condition and the weather, a squirrel will start hibernation sometime between late August and late September. As they sleep through the winter, squirrels remain in a much deeper state of hibernation than bears. The squirrel's body temperature will stay just slightly above the freezing point. Its pulse, breathing and other metabolic processes are barely perceptible. One study found that a squirrel's winter metabolism is only

about 1/200th of its summer rate.

Male squirrels wake from hibernation first, sometime in April. They immediately set out to establish or reestablish breeding territories. Only males with a territory can attract mates, so there is heated competition for the best areas. The females later wake up, investigate the nearby territories, select one and mate with the owner. The young, a litter of four to six, will be born in early June.

Native people used squirrels primarily as sources of fur. They were called "the parka squirrel" because their skins were used to make parkas. (A traditional squirrel skin coat is on display at the University of Alaska Museum in Fairbanks.) At times, natives also used squirrels for food, but they were usually considered to be just an emergency food used only if caribou and salmon were unavailable.

HOARY MARMOTS

The marmot belongs to the same family as the squirrel but grows to a much larger size, perhaps up to 15 to 20 pounds. Marmots have a much smaller population than squirrels because they restrict themselves to rocky talus slopes. Their dens are built under a pile of boulders, rocks that would be too heavy for even a grizzly to move. With persistence, a bear can dig a squirrel out of its shallow tundra burrow, but it is almost impossible to capture a marmot once it has ducked into its rocky fortress.

Marmots are one of the few Denali animals which mate for life and live as family units. The pair will mate every second year on the average and keep their young for at least two full years. Marmots are very social animals and interact with each other frequently. They often greet other family members with what looks like a kiss. The kissing enables them to identify each other by their specific scent. Another common social behavior is a type of play fight where two marmots will meet, stand up, tilt their heads back and wrestle with their front paws. In the fall, the whole family hibernates together in the den.

Two members of a marmot family greet.

PIKAS

A pika collecting grasses to store for the winter.

If you sit down on a rockslide, sooner or later you will hear a high-pitched squeak. Look quickly and you might see the flash of a tiny gray animal darting across the rocks. It might be carrying a bouquet of flowers in its mouth. It may stop, regard you for a moment and then go on its way. This miniature rock sprite is called the pika.

Pikas weigh only a few ounces and average about four inches in length. They always live in rock piles, usually near marmots. The spaces between the rocks provide security as well as places to store their winter food cache. Throughout the summer and fall, pikas diligently collect vast quantities of food and hide them under rocks. When winter snows cover the rock piles and feeding areas, the pikas tunnel under the snow to the caches.

Each pika has its own individual territory and will fight to defend it from any invading neighbor. Their call is primarily used to proclaim territorial ownership, serving the same purpose as a male bird's spring territorial song. The defended territory includes all of a pika's food caches. Feeding and harvesting areas are normally used communally and not defended by individuals. Those areas are shared by the whole pika colony.

BEAVER

B eaver, like marmots, mate for life and keep their young for two years. Unlike marmots, however, they do not hibernate. Instead they collect huge quantities of branches in late summer and early fall for use during the long winter. Once the pond freezes over, the food cache must support the entire family, as many as 10 animals, until spring. If the beaver underestimated the amount of food needed, they might starve to death under the ice.

Many of the beaver in Denali live in places where you might not expect to find them, areas of shrubby brush rather than full-size trees. This is especially true of the beaver ponds located between Eielson Visitor Center and Wonder Lake. The lack of trees forces these beaver to live at the very margin of their ability to survive. After only a few years at a pond, a family may find that they have cut down all the nearby edible vegetation. They must then either range further and further away to find food or abandon the pond. Since beaver are very vulnerable once they leave the water, it is usually safer for them to leave home and start over again in a new location. The family will swim upstream or downstream and hunt for a suitable location for a new dam and pond. After a few years have gone by, the shrubs at the old pond will grow back and a new family may move in and rebuild the dam and lodge.

Left, *small tundra ponds can support a beaver family for only a few years.*

Inset, *a beaver feeds on willow leaves and bark.*

WOLVES

I n Denali, you might hear a sound which is truly the call of the wild: the howl of a wolf. The language of wolves is beyond our ability to understand. We can only guess at the meaning. Perhaps a howling wolf is telling others of its kind where it is, perhaps the wolf is expressing how it feels. The howl may serve the same purpose as human music, conveying both information and emotion. Whatever its meaning, wolf music is a sound which will always echo in your mind.

If you hear a wolf, come across its tracks or see one trotting over the tundra, consider yourself lucky. Few people today have had the privilege of seeing a wild wolf. Wolves once populated places like Yosemite and Yellowstone National Parks but are now long gone from those areas. Denali is one of the few National Parks that has been able to retain its wolf population. Like grizzly bears, wolves require large areas of wilderness to survive. The presence of both grizzlies and wolves in Denali National Park is indisputable proof that the area is basically unchanged from what it was before the coming of civilization to Alaska.

The Denali wolves can range in color from white to black, but most are gray. They might be seen traveling singly or in small groups. If a pack is sighted, look for a wolf with its tail in the air. This will be the alpha male, the leader of the pack. He may not be the first in line, in fact, he may bring up the rear. The alpha wolf sometimes delegates the lead position to the beta male, his second in command. When a challenging situation arises, such as an opportunity to kill a caribou or a confrontation with a rival pack, the alpha wolf will resume command and direct the response of the pack.

In a wolf pack, the only members who breed are the alpha male and the alpha female. Their litter is born in the spring and all members of the pack help to raise the young pups. The other adult wolves are almost always related to the alpha pair as brothers, sisters or previous offspring. Feeding a litter of five to ten pups is a difficult job, even for the entire pack. If all of the pack members tried to breed, the pack's territory could not support the resulting large number of offspring. The pack is better served by limiting breeding to the dominant pair, the wolves who have proven themselves to be the fittest animals.

Day and night, summer and winter, the Denali wolves range across the tundra in a timeless search for prey. Caribou, moose or Dall sheep are the preferred food but ptarmigan, squirrels and other rodents make up a significant portion of their diet. Much of what is now known about wolves was discovered by Adolf Murie, a biologist assigned to the Park in the 1930s to study wolves and their relationship with their prey. He was the first scientist who extensively investigated wolf behavior in the field.

In 1944, Murie published the results of his studies in his book, *The Wolves of Mt. McKinley,* one of the great classics of animal behavior. His book documented that wolves preyed primarily on the sick

*The wolf, sending a musical
message to the rest of his pack.*

and weak Dall sheep and caribou as well as the very young and very old. Healthy animals could normally escape the wolves. He concluded that wolves ultimately helped to keep their prey species in a healthy and strong state. Because of Murie's book, wolves have come to be perceived as animals very different from the fictional wolves of fairytales. Rather than being seen as unmerciful killers, intent on wholesale slaughter, the wolf is now understood to be an important and necessary part of the wilderness, a creature to be cherished and preserved.

DENALI'S BIRDS

At least 158 different species of birds have been spotted in Denali. With few exceptions, these species live in the Park only during the spring and summer months and then leave to migrate south. They come north to take advantage of the eruption of life which occurs on the tundra each spring. The tundra offers a nearly limitless banquet of food (plants, insects and small animals) to birds attempting to raise hungry chicks.

One of Denali's birds, the arctic tern, is the world record holder for long-distance migration. These gull-like birds breed and nest on the shores of tundra ponds. In late summer, the terns and their young start a journey which will eventually take them to the Antarctic. Summer is just beginning in the Southern Hemisphere as the terns arrive. The round-trip flight from Alaska to the Antarctic and back is approximately 25,000 miles!

Other long-distance commuters include the American golden plover, the surfbird, the long-tailed jaeger, the arctic warbler and the wheatear. Some plovers winter on the Hawaiian Islands while others migrate to Argentina. Tierra del Fuego, at the tip of South America, is the winter home of the surfbird. Jaegers spend winters on the open ocean in the central Pacific or near Japan. Arctic warblers reside in places such as Indonesia, the

An arctic tern pauses in the day-long task of fishing to feed its family. Soon the parents and young will begin the long flight to Antarctica.

Philippines and Borneo during winter months. Wheatears traverse the entire continent of Asia to reach their African wintering range.

Willow ptarmigan, the Alaska state bird, live in the Park year round along with their close relatives, the rock and white-tailed ptarmigan. Ptarmigan are brown in summer and white during winter, changing coloration to blend with the natural background. The scientific name for ptarmigan is Lagapus, meaning "rabbit foot." Their legs and feet are covered with dense feathers which resemble the fur on a rabbit's foot. The foot-warming feathers are an ideal adaptation to the winters in the far north. During extremely cold winter weather, ptarmigan insulate themselves by burrowing into snow drifts. In the spring, the males fiercely defend their mates. One male was actually seen attacking a grizzly bear who had stumbled on his mate's nest. Look for ptarmigan in willow thickets and on the open tundra.

Another year-round resident is the raven. Their intelligence and toughness enable them to survive the most extreme climates on the face of the earth, from the Denali winters to the Death Valley summers. Climbers on Denali are frequently robbed of their food by ravens who can easily fly to the 18,000-foot level. The only way to protect a food cache from the wily birds is to bury it under several feet of snow. At first, climbers marked their caches with a red flag but it wasn't long before the ravens figured out the meaning of the flags and learned to dig through the snow to the hidden treasure.

The raven is the greatest and most important character in the stories of the local Athapaskan Indians. They say the earth was made by *Dotson'sa—The Great Raven*. Stories tell how Raven once saved all the other animals when a great flood covered the world and how he later created humans. It is traditional for Athapaskans to pray to ravens for personal luck and hunting success, addressing their requests to *Tseek'all—Old Grandfather*.

Although the raven is viewed as a powerful spirit or god, natives also believe that the birds love to play the role of clown, mischief maker, trickster, and thief. Most of the raven stories emphasize these aspects of the bird's nature. The tales give the impression that the ravens, bored with their great powers, decided to get by through tricking and deceiving other animals and people.

Golden eagles, the darker cousins of the bald eagle, are commonly seen throughout Denali. They primarily hunt rodents such as the arctic ground squirrel but may try to tackle marmots or red foxes. A group of shuttle bus passengers once saw an eagle attempt to carry off a young grizzly cub: the cub was saved by a quick charge by its mother.

Bald eagles are occasionally seen in the Park but are considered rare. Since most of the glacial streams are too silty for fish, the bald eagles do not find the area suitable for their fish-based diet.

Denali's birds can be seen and studied by anyone possessing time and a pair of binoculars. While near tundra ponds look for loons, grebes, geese, ducks, yellow-legs, phalaropes and sandpipers. On tundra watch for long-tailed jaegers, golden plovers, whimbrels, snow buntings, wheatears, sparrows and water pipits. Owls, goshawks, woodpeckers, gray jays and chickadees are common in forested areas. Park rangers, tour bus drivers and shuttle drivers can give you suggestions on how to find specific bird species in Denali National Park.

Above, *a common loon at Wonder Lake. Ground-nesting birds, like the loon, tern and ptarmigan, are common on the tundra.*

Right, *a ptarmigan in its protective winter plumage.*

Denali's red fox are active all winter, feeding on ptarmigan or voles.

By June the snowshoe hare has changed into its brown summer coloration. Its relatively small ears show specialized adaptation to Denali's severe winter climate.

The most exciting way to experience wildlife goes beyond simply spotting them and snapping photos. Try to understand these animals by sitting down on the tundra and really watching them. Set aside a few hours, sit at a distance so that you do not disturb them and quietly observe how Denali's residents live out their lives. The opportunity to have an intimate glimpse into the world of Alaskan wildlife is something you may never have again. Take advantage of it and enter into their world.

CHAPTER FOUR

EXPERIENCING DENALI

Denali National Park is a sacred place: a portion of the pristine Alaskan tundra set aside and preserved in its original state. Denali is a sanctuary for the plants, mammals and birds of the tundra, a living refuge forever wild, forever an island in time.

It is worthwhile to consider what you want to get from your Denali trip. Are you here to check off one more name on your list of National Parks? Did you come to see the mountain and a grizzly bear as quickly as possible so you can go on to the next stop on your itinerary? If these are the reasons for your visit, you may well miss the real Denali.

Experiencing the real Denali takes time. Don't rush things. Make the effort to really look at the mountains, the tundra plants and the wildlife. Try to understand and appreciate Denali and why it is so unique. What you discover may become one of your most unforgettable encounters.

Absorbing the presence of Denali.

VISITOR PROGRAMS

RANGER PROGRAMS

A good way to start understanding Denali is to take part in some of the interpretive programs offered by the National Park Service. Every day, Park Service naturalists present slide shows, campfire talks, nature walks and discovery hikes. Many of the programs take place near the Riley Creek/Hotel area. Other activities, such as the discovery hikes, start at various locations out in the Park. Check at the Park Hotel or at the Visitor Centers for the weekly listing of Park Service programs. The naturalists conducting each program will not only help you learn about Denali, but will also encourage you to seek out an appreciation of the Park through your own personal exploration.

DOG SLEDDING DEMONSTRATIONS

Be sure to visit Denali's sled dog kennel, located behind the Park Headquarters. At the kennel you will personally meet about 30 of the government's hardest-working employees: the sled dogs who help the rangers patrol Denali National Park. All of the dogs are friendly and love to be petted and scratched. During the summer season rangers put on daily dog sledding demonstrations— one of the most popular Park programs.

Left above, *Ranger Kim Heacox leads discovery hikers up the Mt. Healy overlook trail.*

Left below, *Park visitors share the excitement of dog sledding. Most Park sled dogs are born at Denali's kennels and trained by Park Service Staff.*

Above, *highlight of the Tundra Wildlife Tour is Stony Hill Overlook and the first full view of Mt. McKinley at mile 61 on the Park Road.*

WILDLIFE TOUR BUSES

Another way to begin your Denali experience is to participate in one of the Tundra Wildlife Tours sponsored by the Denali Park Hotel. Offering an intensive introduction to the Park and its wildlife, these eight-hour bus tours are conducted by experienced guides who explain and interpret the meaning of the Park to the passengers.

SHUTTLE BUSES

Denali's shuttle bus system has been set up to facilitate your opportunity to have a quality experience while in the Park. The system provides not only basic transportation but also encourages people to get off the buses and explore the Park.

You may leave your bus, hike for a few hours and then return to the road to catch a later bus. Buses will stop to pick up passengers anywhere along the Park road.

The shuttle system was instituted in 1972, the year the Fairbanks-Anchorage Highway was completed. Up to that point, visitation in the Park had been very low: in the five years prior to 1972, the average annual visitation was only 15,000. The Park's remote location and lack of direct access by vehicle combined to limit tourism. When the new highway opened, it became much easier for both tourists and Alaskan residents to reach the Park. In the next five years, visitation jumped to an average of over 140,000 per year, almost a tenfold increase over the previous figures. By 1985, recreational visits reached 435,000!

WALKS AND HIKES

Once you have had a chance to learn some of the basics about Denali, it is time to set out on your own journey of personal discovery. To really know Denali, you must walk the land and experience its beauty at close range. For some, this might begin as a two-hour walk on one of the nature trails near the Hotel. For others, it might take the form of a week-long backpacking trip into the Alaska Range. The locations and details of your Denali adventures are not important. What is important is to actually get out there and experience the Park on its own terms. Get off the road, get away from the campgrounds and visitor centers and discover why Denali is a place set apart, an island in time.

Denali National Park is a true wilderness. Developments and improvements are kept to a minimum. There are only a few official trails, mainly in the entrance area. In the rest of the Park, you are on your own. Despite the vast size of the Denali wilderness, route-making is not difficult. Since most of the Park is open tundra, it is easy to visually choose a destination and hike straight toward it. Many hikers simply walk either up or down one of the numerous rivers which cross the Park road perpendicularly.

Before you begin a day hike, talk to a ranger at Riley Creek or Eielson Visitor Centers about tips on conditions and safety. Maps of the area you will be exploring are available at both Centers. Permits are required for overnight hikes.

Left, *hiking the ridge above Park Headquarters*.

Above, *relaxing on the tundra*.

WATCHING AND PHOTOGRAPHING WILDLIFE

It is probable that your most intense experience while in Denali National Park will be the thrill of seeing a wild grizzly, wolf, caribou or other animal freely roaming about in its natural habitat. Denali is a paradise for watching and photographing wildlife. A pair of binoculars and a telephoto lens will greatly assist you in these activities. This equipment will allow you to observe and photograph the animals from a safe distance and in a way that will usually not disturb them or drive them away.

Remember that some wild animals are dangerous and will attack if provoked. Never approach a grizzly—view them from the protection of a bus or Visitor Center. Always stay well away from a bull moose and a cow with calf. Dall sheep and caribou bulls are fairly tolerant of people if you abide by their rules. Allow them to spot you while you are still a long way from them. It is critical that they have a chance to identify you as a person, rather than a predator. Making sure that you are always in their field of view, approach them at a very slow walk with frequent pauses. Before they exhibit disturbance at your presence sit down and take out your binoculars and camera. This method of approaching wildlike will enable you to watch and study their behavior without causing them unnecessary stress.

Above, *photographing tundra wildflowers.*

Right, *veteran photographer Charlie Ott has been visiting Denali for over 30 years.*

Far right, *the tundra lacks trees, but Denali's bears find these government-provided scratching posts convenient!*

CLIMBING DENALI TODAY

Left, climbing Karstens ridge above the Muldrow Glacier.

Above, a triumphant climber has successfully reached McKinley Peak.

The highest peak on the North American continent, Denali lures many climbers to its slopes. In recent years, as many as 700 people annually have tried to climb the mountain. Most parties ascend on the West Buttress Route, a route on the southwest side of Denali first climbed in the early 1950s. Mountaineers charter planes to take them and their equipment to the 7,000-foot level on the Kahiltna Glacier. From this point, the average party takes two to three weeks to reach the summit and return.

There are many routes to the summit other than the West Buttress, but all are longer and most are considered much more challenging. Usually only experienced climbers attempt the alternate routes.

According to records kept by the National Park Service, only about 50% of Denali's climbers succeed in reaching the summit. Bad weather is the main reason for failure. If a storm strikes while a party is above the 15,000-foot level, the members must either give up and descend or wait for the storm to subside. Since some storms can last for a week, most parties are forced to terminate their trip. Medical problems brought on by the extreme cold, high elevations, low oxygen and the stress of a long expedition also impede climbers and may cause serious accidents as well as fatalities.

THE WILDERNESS SPIRIT OF DENALI

Denali National Park is one of the world's greatest accessible wilderness areas. The Park was set aside so that *you* could come here and experience such sights as a grizzly feeding on blueberries, a wolf pack trotting across the tundra, a caribou herd conducting their never-ending migration, a cow moose nursing her newborn calf, or a band of Dall rams running up a seemingly unclimbable cliff face. These things have occurred in Denali since before there were people to witness them. The purpose of the National Park is to insure that the wildlife and the entire tundra ecosystem be preserved and protected for all time in their original condition.

Denali may be an island in time but we must not complacently think that it is therefore safe from threats which might dilute its wilderness character. Currently, the Park Service is struggling with the problem of overuse of the Park. Should visitation be allowed to increase to the point where the Park is damaged, or should limits be set? Pollution, acid rain and other recent human inventions may soon threaten the integrity of the Denali ecosystem. How can the Park be saved from these dangers originating far outside our boundaries?

Denali National Park is an island in time that needs—and deserves—protection from the intrusions of our modern world. If we can do this, we will pass on an inheritance to our grandchildren and their descendants far more valuable than mere money or possessions. Preserving the legacy of the Denali wilderness is a mission that is worthy of our best efforts.

Adolf Murie, the biologist who spent 25 summers in Denali, once wrote of his feelings about the Park. He concluded his book *A Naturalist in Alaska* with these words: ". . . it is not only the outward beauty of Alaska that we must think about when considering its future; we must think of its native wildness—its wilderness spirit. This we cannot improve. The problem is to preserve it."

On the Muldrow Glacier.

Denali National Park Alaska